I know I Can!
Wash the Dishes

ANTHEA DAVIDSON-JARRETT

Illustrated by

Aldana Penayo

Published by EDUCATE THE GLOBE,
London, UK, 2023.

ISBN: 978-1-913804-09-1

Copyright © 2022 Educate The Globe Limited. All rights reserved. No part of this book is to be reprinted, copied or stored in retrieval systems of any type, except by written permission from the author. Part of this book may, however, be used only in reference to support related documents or subjects.

I know I can do it!
Please can I help?
I want to do it all by myself!

Please can I try?
Can you show me how?
I'm not too small.
I am ready right now!

We've had Sunday dinner
and we're all full up!
Time to clear the table
and do the washing-up.

Mummy cooked dinner.
Daddy made dessert.
It's our job to wash dishes;
that's how it works!

Scrape off the food into the compost bin. Make sure you watch what you're doing!

Drain any liquids down the sink. Nasir helps me do it so I don't break anything.

Fill all the pots
with soapy hot water.
Leave the pots until last -
this is our preferred order.

Now we fill the sink
with hot sudsy water.
Mummy shouts not to break
the dishes that daddy bought her!

Soak the glasses in
their steamy bath –
take care when you do it;
no time for shattered glass!

Set them aside
in the next door sink
or next to each other
on the side of the sink.
Use a tea towel
so the water doesn't leak
all over the counter and
into next week.

Now we wash the cutlery
with a sponge or a brush.
Take your time, do it attentively.
There's no need to rush!

Be careful with the knives;
we don't want a horror scene.
I think I'm washing better than the
dish washing machine!

Set the cutlery down
right next to the glasses.
A soapy bubbly party is exactly
what this task is!

Time to wash the plates now remove the muck and the grease. Scrub-a dub-dub until they're squeaky clean.

Set the plates with the glasses and the cutlery. This is how we do it but it's not compulsory.

Now pull out the plug and
insert the plug strainer
so any food left behind doesn't
block the pipes later.

Now we have everything
stacked in a pile.
Time to rinse them off –
we'll finish in no time!

Empty the sink –
plug and fill it once more.
No soap this time just
water that is warm.

Place everything gently in the drainer to dry. Time to wash the pots. It's elbow grease time!

Use the scourer for the pots
or the rough brillo pad.
This part is tough...
"Please help me dad!"

Rinse the pots out with water.
Dad will put them away.
Dry everything on the drainer
and then we'll put them away.

Washing-up is fun
I could do this every day.
But now it's all done so
it's time to play!

www.ingramcontent.com/pod-product-compliance
Lightning Source LLC
Chambersburg PA
CBHW041244240426
43670CB00027B/2988